JHANSI KI RANI LAKSHMIBAI

Om KIDZ
An imprint of Om Books International

First Published in 2024 by

Om KIDZ | Om Books International

Corporate & Editorial Office
A-12, Sector 64, Noida 201 301
Uttar Pradesh, India
Phone: +91 120 477 4100
Email: editorial@ombooks.com
Website: www.ombooksinternational.com

Sales Office
107, Ansari Road, Darya Ganj
New Delhi 110 002, India
Phone: +91 11 4000 9000
Email: sales@ombooks.com

ISBN: 978-93-53769-16-1

Printed in India

10 9 8 7 6 5 4 3 2 1

Contents

Rani Lakshmibai 5
The History of Bundelkhand 6
A Queen Is Born 10
Manu's Games and Sports 14
Elephants for Royalty 20
Manu Gets Married 34
A Son Is Born 52
Sorrow and Tragedy 56
The Doctrine of Lapse 60
A Son Is Adopted 62
Gangadhar Rao's Letter 65
Demise of Gangadhar Rao 68
Dalhousie Refuses the Request 74
Rani Lakshmibai's Life Changes 76
Jhansi Mistreated 92
The Durga Dal 101
False Blame 106
Ready for Battle 111
The Fearsome Battle 116
A Hero Dies 122

Rani Lakshmibai

Rani Lakshmibai was the Queen of Jhansi, who contributed to the First War of Indian Freedom. She courageously fought several battles against the British. She was just twenty-nine years old when she died fighting in a battle. We remember her today because of her patriotism, determination and heroism. She is compared to Saint Joan of Arc, another woman whose name is etched in history for her display of valour and fearlessness.

The History of Bundelkhand

The city of Jhansi situated between the rivers Betwa and Pahuj was a part of Bundelkhand in ancient times and ruled by Chandela kings. But with the decline of the Chandelas, Jhansi lost its importance in the 11th century. Its glory was somewhat restored in the 17th century when Raja Bir Singh Deo of Orccha built the Jhansi Fort in 1613. He had good relations with the Mughal Emperor Jahangir.

Thereafter, many Rajas or Bundela Sardars, as they were known, succeeded the throne.

Mughal Emperor Aurangzeb ascended the throne of Delhi in 1658. He was a tyrant, who wanted to claim his hold over most of the region. However, to Aurangzeb's astonishment his forceful armies lost to Chhatrasal. Thus, peace prevailed in the Bundelkhand land for a long period of time till 1732.

With Chhatrasal growing old and weak, the Mughals decided to attack Bundelkhand again. However, the wise Chhatrasal joined hands with the Maratha Peshwa and once again defeated the Mughal army. This alliance proved fruitful to the Marathas, as the old Chhatrasal gifted one third of his territory to Peshwa Baji Rao I, as a token of thanks for their help. Jhansi, too, was under the gifted territory, thereby, it came under the rule of the Marathas.

In 1803 a treaty was signed between the East India company and Marathas. Raghunath Rao became the subedar of Jhansi in 1835 but he died in 1838. After ruling Jhansi efficiently for many years, he was succeeded by his brother Shivaram Bhau. Thereafter, the Maratha power declined. Shivaram Bhau ruled by establishing friendly relationships with the British.

After his death, Shivaram Bhau's grandson Ramachandra Rao succeeded the throne. He served the British with great sycophancy and emptied his treasury in pleasing them. The Rajput rulers of Orchha and Datia could not bear to see him rule Jhansi so badly. They killed him in a battle while he was just 29 years old.

It was now, with the Jhansi treasury below the 3-lakh mark and the administration scattered that the British took a quick decision to throne Gangadhar Rao, as the new King of Jhansi. It was this man who provided infinite encouragement to his legendary wife Lakshmibai, the Rani of Jhansi! Raja Gangadhar Rao was a very good administrator. He was very generous and full of sympathy. and the local population of Jhansi was very satisfied.

A Queen Is Born

The city of Kashi (now known as Varanasi) was inhabited by 30,000 Maratha Brahmin families in the 19th century. The Tambe family belonged to the class of Maratha Brahmins who had immigrated to Kashi from Satara. Balwant Rao Tambe, the son of a soldier from the Peshwa army settled in Kashi with his two sons, Moropant and Sadashiv. Moropant was married to Bhagirathi Bai, a beautiful lady who was well-versed in Hindu Scriptures. Soon, this wonderful couple was blessed with a lovely daughter.

The baby was born in the month of November, in the city of Kashi. The exact year and time of her birth are not known. She was named Manikarnika, or Manu. When Manu was just a toddler, her mother died, leaving her in the care of her loving father, who held an important position in the court of Peshwa Baji Rao II of Bithoor. Moropant moved to Bithoor. Manu began to participate in the games and sports that the princes indulged in. Thus, because of her father's position, Manu spent her childhood among the boys of the palace.

The Peshwa was very fond of Manu. She was a spritely girl and the palace reverberated with her energy and innocent prattle.

The Peshwa fondly nicknamed her Chhabeeli. Chhabeeli is another name for the Mynah bird, who is chirpy and is full of life, just the way little Manu was. Manu was humble like her father, playful like the boys in the palace and religious like her mother.

In those times, not many girls were educated, as they stayed indoors and helped with the household work. However, Manu learned to read and write. She was a bright student and learnt Sanskrit and Persian, which was the court language. She was always bold, outspoken and very independent.

She always believed that she was equal to any boy. She was very fond of enacting the Ramlila, the story of King Rama. She would often enact the role of Hanuman.

Manu's Games and Sports

Manu rode horses, played war sports, wielded lance and sword and practised rifle shooting since her childhood days.

However, some people did not approve that Manu played games that the princes indulged in. They would complain to her father, that it was not proper for Manu to play such games and sports.

However, Peshwa Baji Rao supported Manu and encouraged her. Manu's father, Moropant Tambe, too,

was never strict with her. Sometimes he would lovingly tell Manu, "You must behave like other girls and play with them."

Manu would reply, “Why? Girls are no less than boys. I will not only play with boys, but defeat them in sports too!” Her father had nothing to say to this!

Meanwhile, many courtiers would complain to Baji Rao, “Moropant doesn’t discipline his daughter Manu.”

However, Baji Rao always supported Moropant, who was an honest and loyal man.

Even while playing among the girls, Manu showed a streak for leadership. She would always play the Queen and all her mates, who did not fulfil her wishes, were fined or punished. She always dealt with them with authority. These early incidents even at this young age clearly reflected her immense ability to rule over a kingdom.

Elephants for Royalty

Besides imbibing qualities from her role models, Manu was extremely honest and upright from childhood. This is evident from another incident from her life. One evening, just after the rainy season, Baji Rao's adopted son Nana Sahib, his younger brother, Rao Sahib and

Manu were riding horses along the banks of the River Ganga. They were all racing their horses. Even though each rider pushed his horse to the utmost, Manu was ahead of the others. Once, Nana Sahib's horse overtook her's. However, she urged her horse to gallop faster and overtook him. Nana would not accept defeat and so tried to overtake her, but his horse stumbled and he fell down.

"O Manu, I am injured. Help me!" he pleaded.

Manu heard the painful cry and rode back, at once. Nana had been hurt and was bleeding. She helped him get up and made him sit on her horse.

Rao Sahib also joined them and they returned to the palace.

Meanwhile, when Nana Sahib's horse returned without the rider, Baji Rao II, the Peshwa of the Maratha Empire, was quite disturbed.

Although Moropant tried to calm him, he was worried for the children. Just then, his children returned and he breathed a sigh of relief.

The men saw Nana Sahib hurt and Moropant said, "Oh, Manu, how unfortunate! Nana has been seriously hurt."

"No. Father, it is only a small wound. Wasn't Abhimanyu seriously injured, yet he continued to fight?"

"That was a different age, Manu," Moropant replied.

"What is the difference, Father? The sky, the earth, the sun and even the moon, are all the same as they were then!"

Besides, making such wise statements, Manu also reprimanded Nana Sahib for raising such a hue and cry over such a small injury.

Later that night, Manu sat talking with her father. She said to him, "Father, Nana Sahib was crying over such a small fall. In my life I will show courage and never hide or shirk away from my duties in times of any problem. I will face all the troubles that come into my life with grit and firmness." This made Moropant Tambe very proud of his little girl.

Once, Baji Rao's sons, Nana Sahib and his two brothers, were going for an elephant ride. Baji Rao also invited Manu to join them in the ride. However, Nana Sahib wanted to take revenge on Manu for she had scolded him and called him weak for crying over the fall from the horse. So, Nana Sahib left for the elephant ride without her.

Manu became very angry with Nana Sahib and demanded that he come back for her. Moropant tried to calm her down, but Manu would not listen at all to him. All his efforts were in vain!

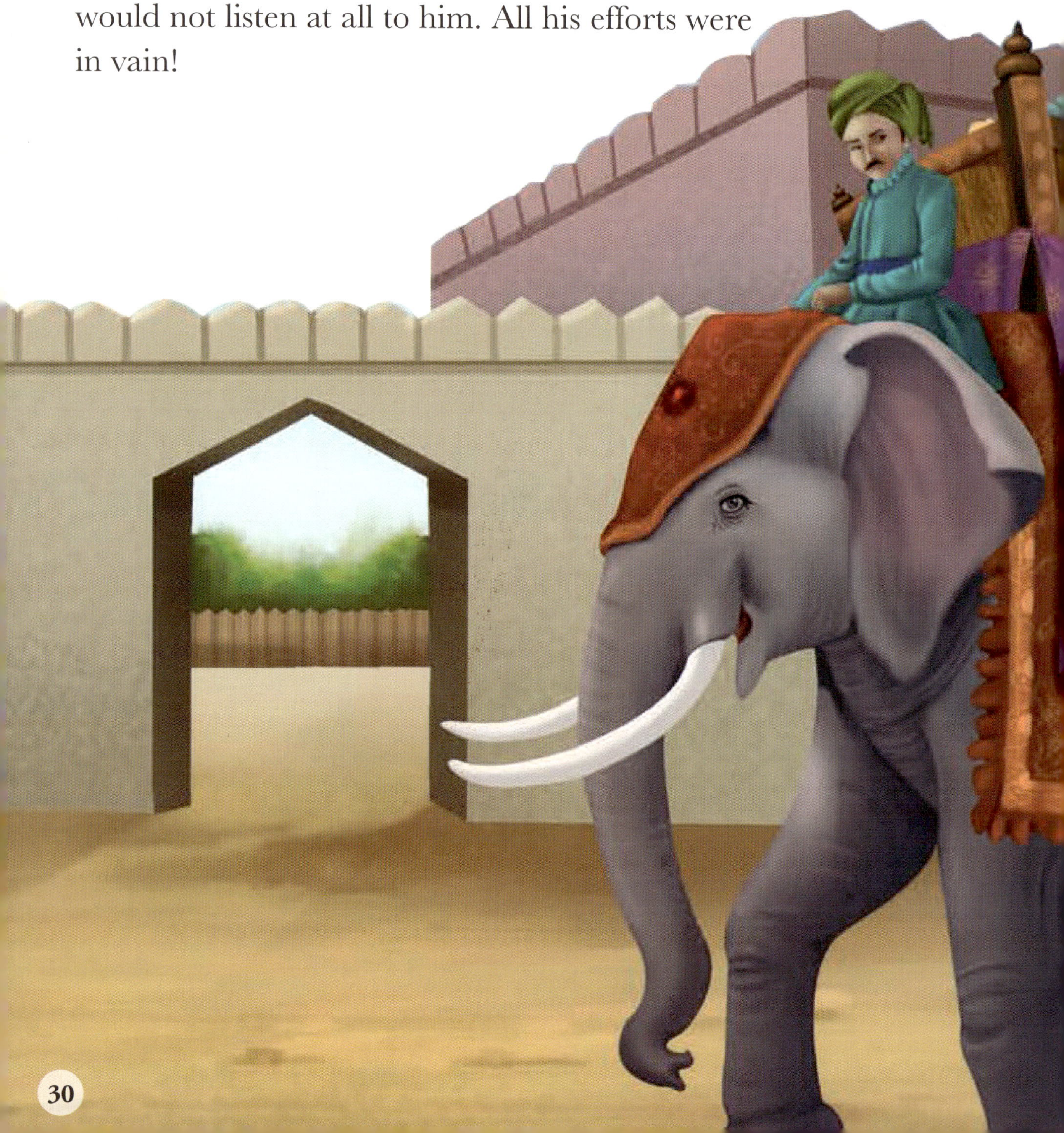

"I want to ride the elephant, too!" she exclaimed.

"No, my child," her father reasoned, "you are not a king's daughter. Only the royal family rides elephants."

Manu did not accept Moropant's reasoning. Her eyes shone with anger, as she said, "Wait till I grow up, Father, I will have ten elephants to ride. Then everyone will see!"

Her father just smiled with affection at his daughter. Little did he know that his precious daughter would grow up to be the Rani of Jhansi, with not just ten, but many elephants at her command.

As Manu grew up, Moropant taught her many lessons from the lives and the examples of the saintly Sita, the brave Jeejabai and Tarabai. Manu learned her lessons well. These strong and virtuous Indian women from the past became her role models.

Manu Gets Married

Time flew by and Manikarnika grew up to be a bright and charming girl. Her father's friends and relatives urged him to get Manu married, for she was now a teenager; whereas, in those times, girls would be married when they were just eight years old. All of them blamed Moropant for neglecting his duty towards Manu. Moropant was very worried, as he wanted a perfect match for Manu. Soon, Manikarnika received a wonderful offer of marriage.

The elders of the kingdom of Jhansi in Bundelkhand, were looking for a bride for their king, Gangadhar Rao.

Gangadhar Rao had been crowned the king, after a great tussle with his stepbrothers and after facing opposition from his stepmother, Sakhubai. When he came to the throne, the kingdom was in a mess. He took help from the British, who had then become powerful in India.

Gangadhar used his intelligence and British help to make his kingdom a flourishing one. He had once been married to Ramabai, who had passed away. Since he had no heir to succeed to the throne after him, it was decided that he should marry again.

At this time, Tantiya Dikshit, a renowned pandit and courtier in Gangadhar's court, came to Bithoor to look for a wife for Gangadhar. When Moropant learnt about his arrival, he took Manu's horoscope to show him, eager to know when Manu would be married.

As Tantiya Dikshit read Manikarnika's horoscope, he knew at once that he had found the future Queen of Jhansi. "This girl is born to be a Queen. Who is she?" he asked.

Surprised, Moropant replied, "She is my daughter."

Tantiya Dikshit asked to meet the girl. Just as he set his eyes on the lovely Manu, he asked Moropant for her hand for Gangadhar Rao, instantly. He obtained permission from the king for this and soon Manikarnika, at the age of fourteen, was married to Gangadhar Rao and became the Queen of Jhansi.

Young Manu was very happy to know that she would now have many impressive elephants in her stable.

The wedding ceremony took place in Jhansi. At that time, it was a custom to change a girl's name once she was married. Thus, Manikarnika's name was changed to Lakshmibai, in reverence to the Goddess Mahalakshmi whom the rulers of Jhansi worshipped as their family deity.

There was an incident that spoke of Lakshmibai's bold and strong nature. It was said that on the day of her wedding, Lakshmibai was not shy or quiet like all Indian brides. Rather she was strong and outspoken. Surprisingly, she even spoke openly during the ceremonies. The guests were especially amazed at one single incident. During the wedding, the priest was tying the knot between Manu and Gangadhar Rao. Just then, Manu said loudly, "Tie the knot tight!" Everybody present laughed out loud.

However, the wise understood that through this sentence, Lakshmibai had demonstrated her clarity of mind and purpose. It spoke of her strong belief and respect for the Indian customs and rituals. In addition, it also stated the fact that Lakshmibai acknowledged to live by her husband's side till death. She knew the sanctity of the relationship between a man and his wife.

Despite her outspoken nature, Lakshmibai left a profound impact on every individual she met. Her honesty and concern was admired and loved by all.

As Lakshmibai started living in Jhansi, the people were surprised to see how bold their Queen was. She continued her riding and fencing practice. Moreover, she involved many women of the palace to exercise with her. She also trained many of them to ride horses and fight with arms. However, along with this, she also fulfilled all her wifely duties. She could cook very well and perform religious rituals perfectly. When her husband made her in-charge of the palace library, she attained academic knowledge, too. The Bhagwad Gita is said to be Lakshmibai's favourite book.

Lakshmibai ruled gracefully as the Queen. From being a free bird as a child, flitting around laughing, she became a decorous, gracious and thoughtful Queen. She had grown up almost overnight. However, young Lakshmibai was sad, as for the first time in her life, she was far away from her father. Gangadhar Rao understood this and invited Moropant to stay in Jhansi. Moropant gladly came to be near his daughter. He built a temple for Lord Krishna in Jhansi and started living there as its priest. Around the same time, Moropant married Chimabai, a calm and intelligent girl, who was Lakshmibai's age. The stepmother and daughter respected each other and soon became good friends.

In her appearance, too, Lakshmibai changed from being a tomboy to an elegant and well-dressed young woman. She dressed carefully and always appeared perfectly groomed in the best of jewellery and beautiful chanderi sarees. She always appeared pleasant and happy, performing her duties as wife and Queen with perfection. Along with various other festivals, she also celebrated the Haldi-Kumkum ceremony after Gauri Puja, with all the women of her city.

It is believed that Lakshmibai assisted her husband in the court. She was an intelligent woman and keenly interested in the affairs of the State. Gangadhar Rao was a patron of arts. He had a fascinating royal theatre, which he managed himself. He was fond of classical singing and dancing, theatre and literature. He would arrange many great performances at his theatre. Thus, many artists and performers would flock to Jhansi, certain of a warm welcome from the King. The King would certainly welcome them and offered them all the luxuries. Lakshmibai, however, was not interested in the arts. She believed it was an unreal world of make-believe and imagination.

"I like to deal with the real life, with the affairs of the State and the problems of our kingdom and subjects," she often told her husband, when they discussed about art.

When Gangadhar saw that Lakshmibai was capable enough to handle Jhansi, he left the work of the State to her, and devoted all his time to the arts.

A Son Is Born

The birth of a son is an auspicious occasion in every Indian family, the royal family in particular. For, then, the throne would have the rightful heir. Thus, it was an occasion of greatest happiness for

Jhansi, when Queen Lakshmibai gave birth to a son.

Gangadhar Rao was very happy. He had the palace decorated with lights, and the occasion was celebrated throughout the kingdom of Jhansi. People joyfully welcomed their baby prince. Many singing and dancing programmes were organised and people from far away were called to join the festivities.

Rani Lakshmibai of Jhansi was the happiest mother. She loved her newborn son and from being a queen and a wife, she expertly glided into the role of a devoted and loving mother for her little son.

However, fate was cruel to Raja Gangadhar Rao and Rani Lakshmibai. The happiness in the palace was very short-lived.

Sorrow and Tragedy

The greatest sorrow for parents is the death of their baby. The King and Queen of Jhansi were devastated, when their infant son, whom they had named Damodar Rao, died, unexpectedly. He had not survived for more than three months. Jhansi plunged into sorrow. The people mourned the death of not just their Prince but also their heir, the hope of their future.

The death of little Damodar changed the fate of Jhansi. From a flourishing, confident and secure kingdom, with the passing away of the young heir, Jhansi transformed into a kingdom without a successor, as there was no heir to the throne now.

The question was, who would be the King of Jhansi after Gangadhar Rao? Everybody believed that the British would now take Jhansi away. This belief was rooted in a law made by Lord Dalhousie.

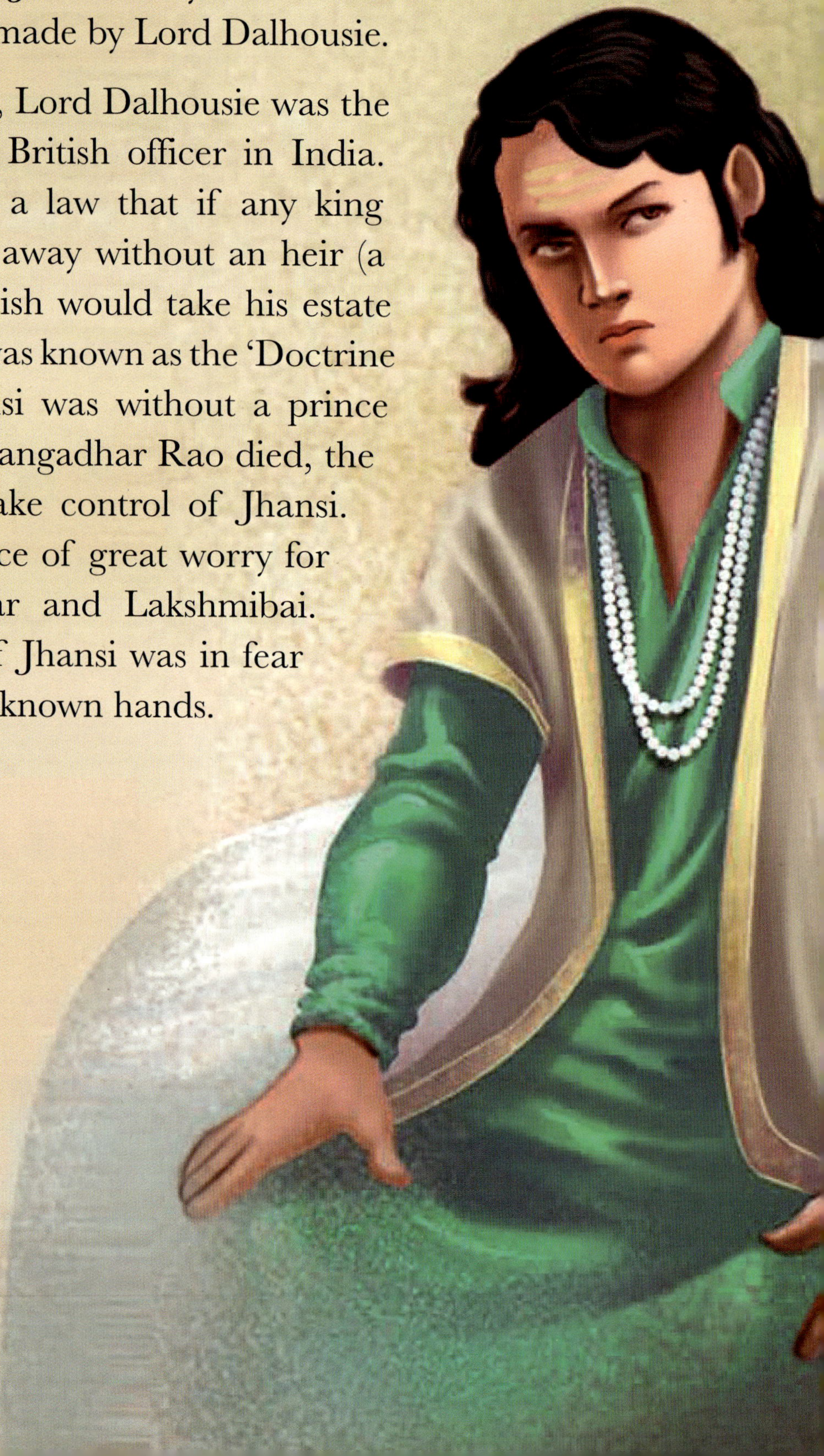

At that time, Lord Dalhousie was the highest-ranking British officer in India. He had passed a law that if any king in India passed away without an heir (a prince), the British would take his estate away. This law was known as the 'Doctrine of Lapse'. Jhansi was without a prince now, so when Gangadhar Rao died, the British would take control of Jhansi. This was a source of great worry for both Gangadhar and Lakshmibai. The kingdom of Jhansi was in fear of going into unknown hands.

The Doctrine of Lapse

Of all the Governor Generals who wielded power over powerful Indian territories, Lord Dalhousie was the most fierce and ambitious. He had organised a special army, wherein, he enrolled only the best soldiers and attacked Burma with immense force.

After raiding Burma his first attack in India was in Oudh. He was successful due to the weak management and disharmony among the Nawab rulers. However, it was not the fearsome battles of Dalhousie but it was his Doctrine of Lapse that crippled the Indian administration.

As per the Doctrine, all Hindu rulers without a natural heir to the throne would have to submit their territory to the British. While no objection was raised against this move in the British Parliament, the doctrine fetched Lord Dalhousie a fat amount of money. Blinded by greed, Lord Dalhousie went on a violent plan of annexing states by all methods. The first kingdom to fall prey to this doctrine was Satara, followed by Jaitpur and Sambalpur in 1849. Dalhousie's next target was Jhansi, as it was a store of great wealth.

A Son is Adopted

However, quite soon, Gangadhar and Lakshmibai adopted a son, a five-year-old boy from their own community. They named him Damodar Rao, after their own son. They thought Jhansi would be safe now, because there was a Prince to claim the throne and take over the rule of Jhansi after Gangadhar Rao. To ensure that the British did not raise an issue over the adoption, Lakshmibai made the local British representatives witness this adoption.

Happiness and good cheer spread in Jhansi again. Rani Lakshmibai and Raja Gangadhar Rao were very happy. However, only time would tell what would be the fate of Jhansi. Everyone was worried for they wondered if the British would accept Damodar Rao as the son of Rani Lakshmibai and Raja Gangadhar Rao. If they did so, Jhansi was safe. If they did not, the fate of Jhansi was ruined. Raja Gangadhar Rao did not know what to do. Confused, he wrote a letter to Lord Dalhousie.

Gangadhar Rao's Letter

Gangadhar Rao wrote a letter to Dalhousie, requesting him not to take over the kingdom of Jhansi, as they had an adopted son. In the letter, he gave all the details about the adoption and requested the East India Company to accept their adopted son as their heir. He suggested that, till Damodar Rao came of age, Rani Lakshmibai should be recognised as the ruler of Jhansi. The Maharaja reminded the Company of the friendly relations between Jhansi and the Company. Gangadhar Rao reminded them of his loyal services to the British and requested them to be merciful.

The letter was handed over by the Maharaja to Major Ellis, with a request to give it to Lord Dalhousie.

Gangadhar Rao told the Major, "Major Sahib, my Rani is a woman. But she is endowed with many qualities, which even the ablest men of the world would admire." As he was speaking, his eyes brimmed with tears.

"Major Sahib, please see that Jhansi does not become on orphan, without an heir and a ruler." he said.

Demise of Gangadhar Rao

Gangadhar Rao was much older than Lakshmibai. He had seen much sadness and hardship in his life. However, since his infant son passed away, Gangadhar was no more a strong and happy man. He was very sad and became ill. He was always worried that Jhansi would be taken over by the British. Gangadhar Rao's condition worsened and he was soon bedridden.

A British doctor, Doctor Allen, came to attend upon him. But the Raja refused to take the medicines, as he was a strict Brahmin and would not take medicine from an impure man who ate meat. Moropant suggested that the medicine could be mixed with *Gangajal*, but the king still refused.

All this while, Lakshmibai sat by her husband's sickbed and nursed him, day and night.

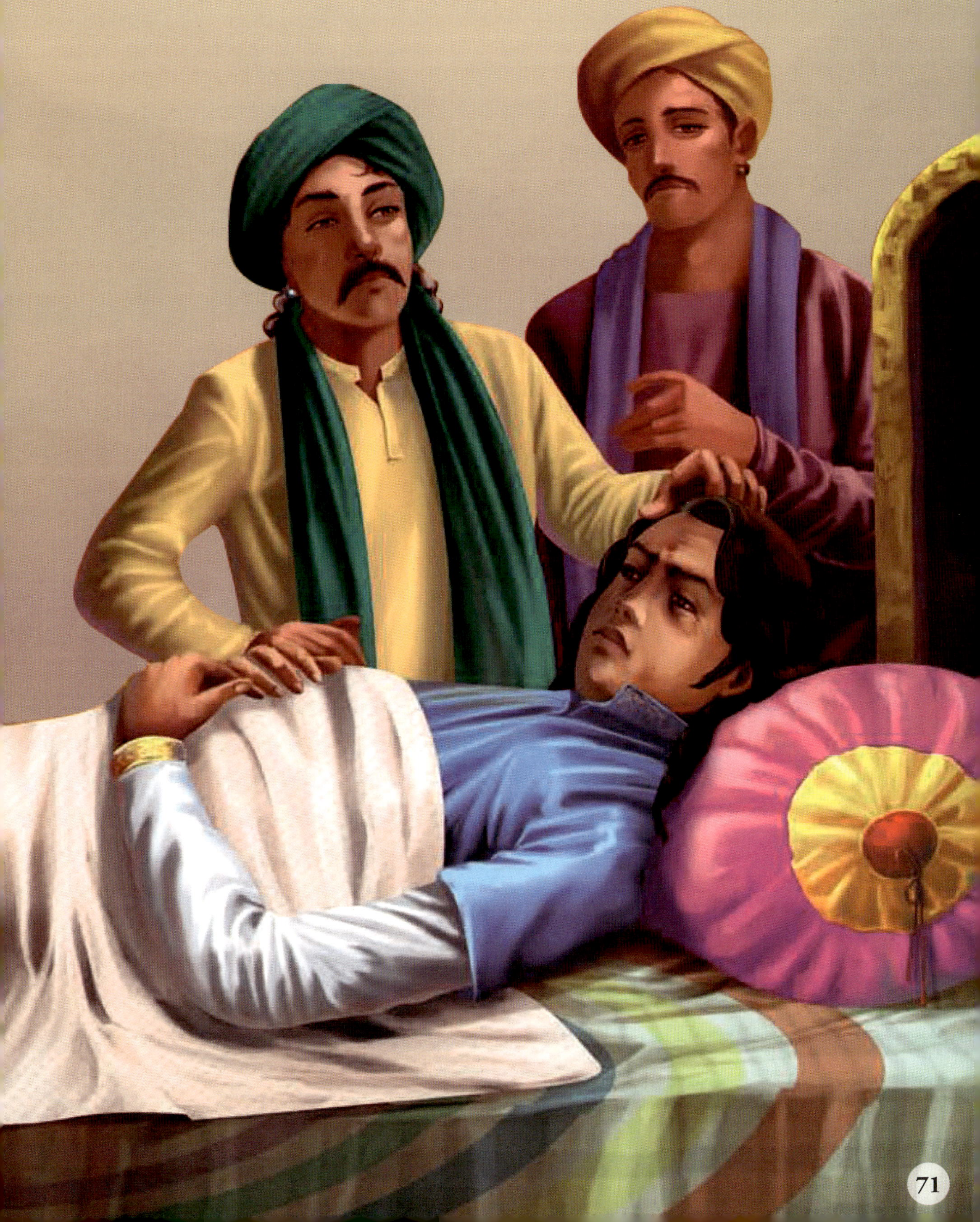

Finally, the moment came and Gangadhar Rao asked for *Gangajal.* He knew he was going to die. And according to the Hindu belief, one who drinks *Gangajal* just before dying, goes to heaven.

Gangadhar passed away after sipping *Gangajal* from his wife's hands. Lakshmibai broke down with grief and sobbed beside her husband. The kingdom drowned in sorrow.

Dalhousie Refuses the Request

Lakshmibai faced the biggest challenge in her life. On one hand, Dalhousie was waiting to take over the kingdom. On the other, Damodar Rao was very young and needed her support and protection. However, she remained strong. She sent a number of letters to Dalhousie for a decision on the Maharaja's letter of request. Three months passed, but there was no reply.

On one unfortunate day in March 1854, Dalhousie's order arrived. The order from Dalhousie read: *The Company does not recognise the right of the Late Maharaja Gangadhar Rao to adopt an heir. It has, therefore, been decided to merge Jhansi into the British provinces. The Rani should vacate the fort and live in the palace situated in the city. She will be paid a monthly pension of rupees five thousand.*

The Kingdom of Jhansi came under the British rule with this order.

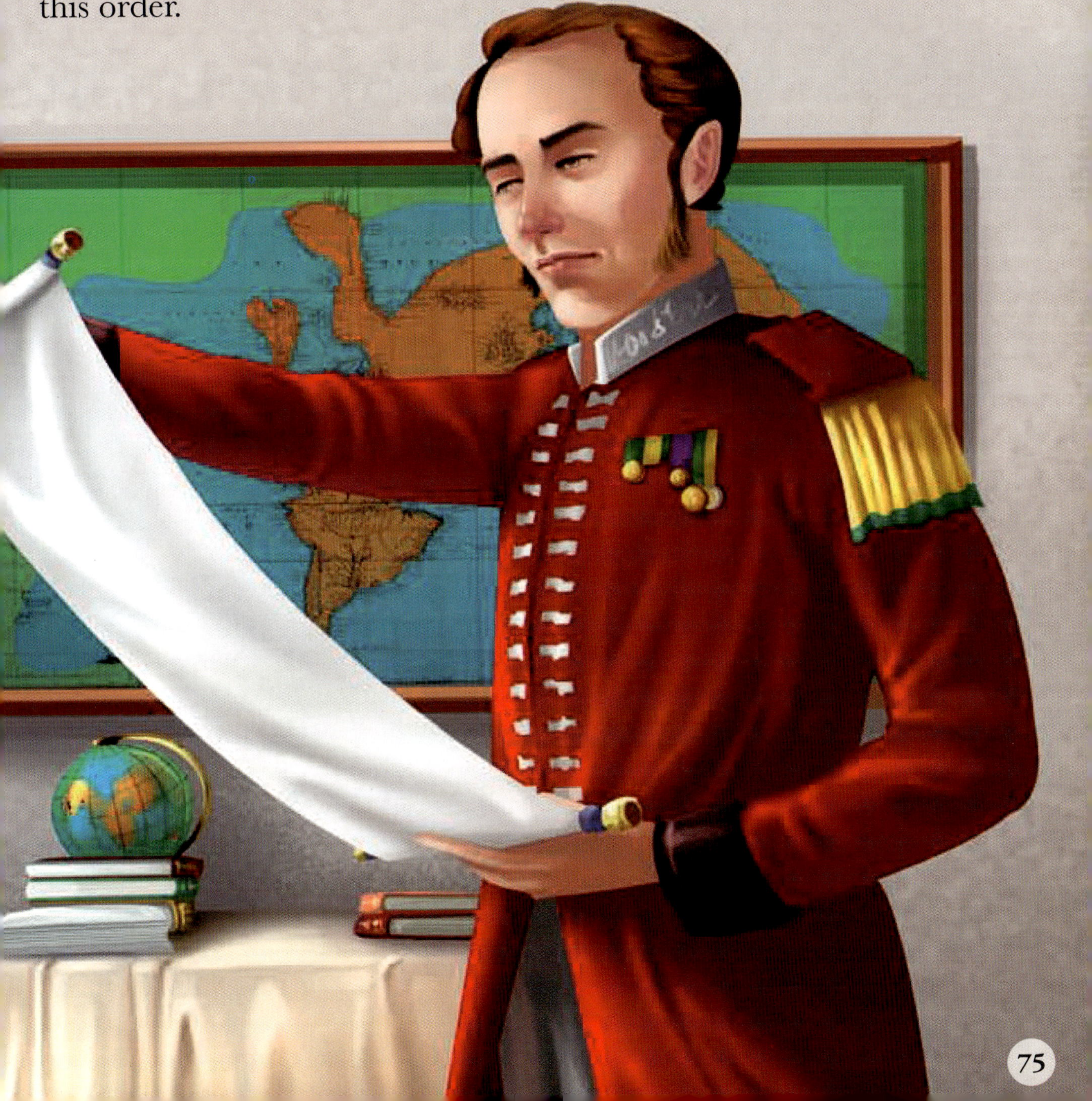

Rani Lakshmibai's Life Changes

The Rani protested the decision of the Company. She wrote a letter to Dalhousie. In the letter, she described the events before her husband died, how he had performed all the necessary rites for adoption of Damodar Rao as their son and the next Raja of Jhansi.

In the Hindu custom, an adopted son is like a natural son. The adopted son can perform all rituals for the family, just like a natural son. The British knew this, but still did not recognise Damodar Rao as Rani Lakshmibai's son, because they wanted to take over Jhansi by fair means or foul.

Some British officers were in favour of Rani Lakshmibai. They tried to convince Dalhousie, but he was not prepared to listen to anyone. All he wanted was to make Jhansi a part of the British Empire. They had annexed many other Indian States by foul means, and thus, expanded their rule over India. The British did not want to lose this opportunity to take over Jhansi.

For, they knew that they could earn more revenue with Jhansi in their hands. It was because of their greed for the wealth of India, that the British made cruel laws. Then, based on these laws, they annexed Indian States without fighting any battle.

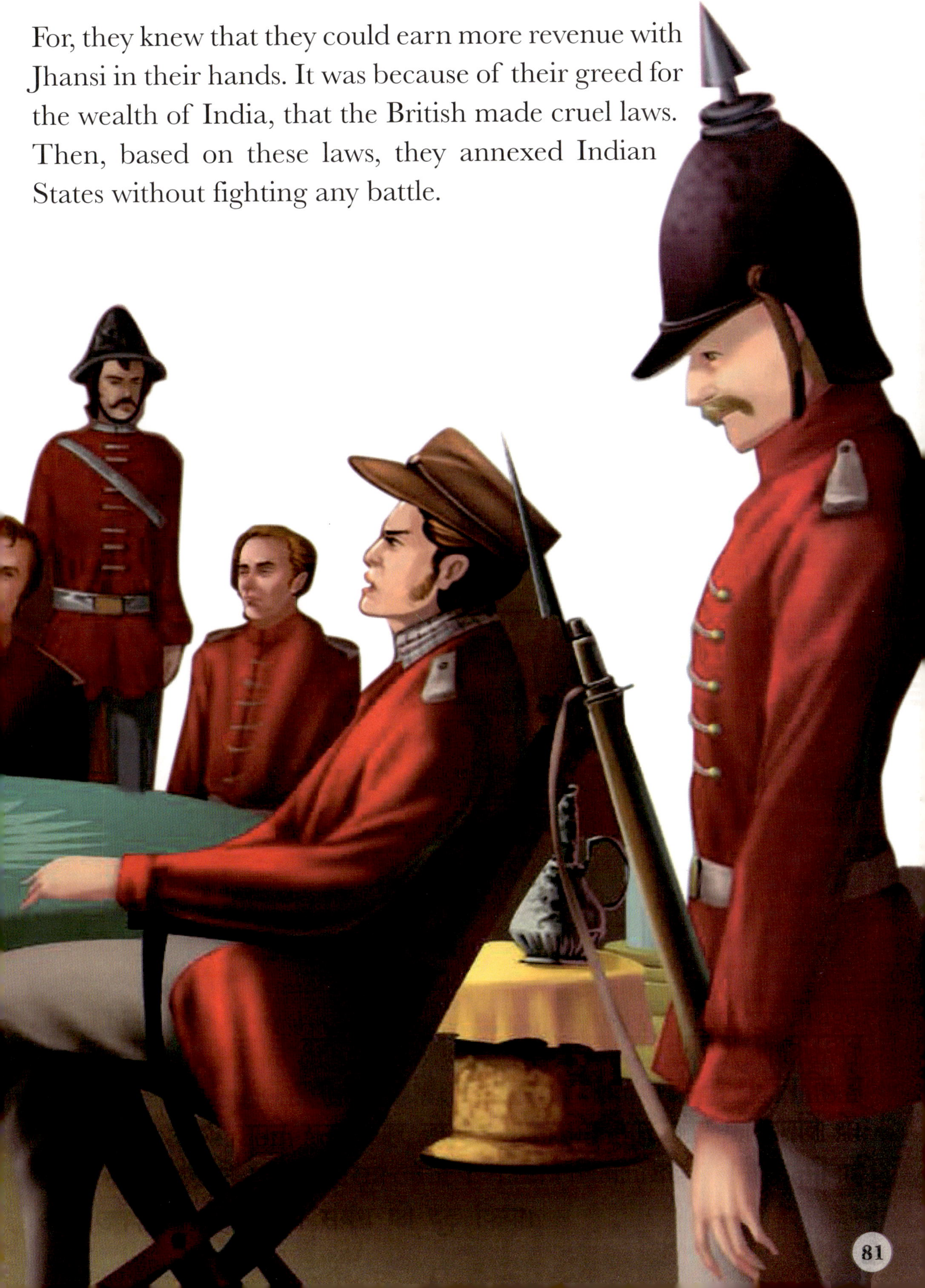

The British were adamant to capture Jhansi. They had taken over all other Indian States, but Jhansi was one of the three States, which were yet to be captured. When Dalhousie refused Raja Gangadhar Rao's request, Rani Lakshmibai pleaded with the British, but they again, refused to see any reason. They wanted her to surrender the fort. When Rani Lakshmibai learned that the British had denied her the right to rule Jhansi, she said determinedly, "I will not give up my Jhansi!"

These words are recorded in history, as they reveal the courage of Indian women in the face of adversity. The words reverberated in Jhansi as they reflected the love and affection Rani Lakshmibai had for her kingdom and the people. This plain statement acted as an adhesive that strengthened the bond between Rani Lakshmibai and her subjects.

A Hindu widow had to follow some basic rules in those days. She had to be clad in a white sari all the time, shave her head, wear no ornaments and live like a recluse. Under the influence of the Mughals, the *Parda* (veil) system had also become prevalent in India. However, Rani Lakshmibai did not follow all these norms. She kept her hair long, donned her colourful saris, wore her jewellery and did not follow the *Parda* rule. But on rare occasions, when she would communicate directly with the British officials, she would wear a *Parda* as a diplomatic move.

Even though she did not follow the superficial regulations expected of a widow, the Rani respected the spiritual requirements from a widow. Thus, her daily routine changed completely. She would get up early in the morning and after her bath, she would devote herself to prayer and meditation. Rani Lakshmibai would devote four hours, from four to eight every morning, to prayers, as was expected of a Hindu widow during her days.

But Rani Lakshmibai's life changed after the administration of Jhansi was taken over by the British. Rani Lakshmibai even shifted to the palace. She followed a strict time-table, but continued practising horse-riding, shooting with guns and arrows and swordsmanship.

Throughout all this, Rani Lakshmibai did not stop her preparation for the battle. From eight to eleven every morning, she would go out on a horse. There, she would practise

shooting with guns and arrows. In the afternoons, she rested for a while. After that, she would exercise lightly in the evening. Later, she would read some religious books and hear religious sermons. Then, she worshipped her chosen deity and had supper. All things were done methodically, according to a strict time-table. She was very disciplined in every aspect of her life. Maybe, maybe that is the reason why she was such an expert and skilful soldier. For, she understood that no battle could be won without clarity and focus.

Despite living such a disciplined life it was getting tougher and tougher for Rani Lakshmibai to maintain her calm and remain quiet. Jhansi was in turmoil. Lakshmibai was aware of the fact that her subjects were living in fear and insecurity of life, money and property. She began to feed the hungry, give alms to the poor and only then eat her food. It was known from some of her close assistants that Rani Lakshmibai would often cry in her living quarters. She was anguished and pained at the thought of losing Jhansi, the memory of her deceased husband and son. She found herself helpless and weak to amass strength to fight against Lord Dalhousie's order.

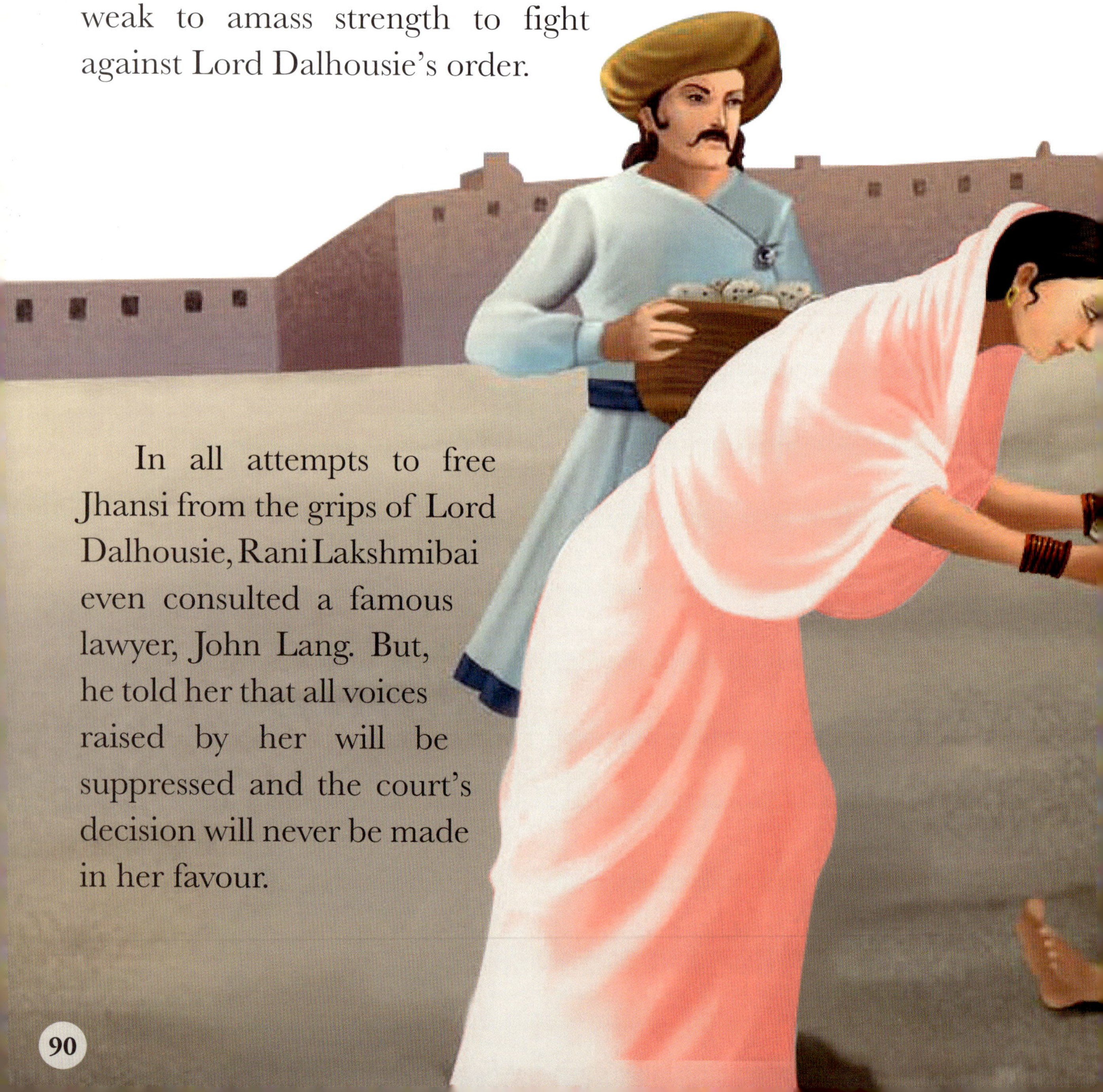

In all attempts to free Jhansi from the grips of Lord Dalhousie, Rani Lakshmibai even consulted a famous lawyer, John Lang. But, he told her that all voices raised by her will be suppressed and the court's decision will never be made in her favour.

Jhansi Mistreated

The Queen and the kingdom of Jhansi had to suffer many insults at the hands of the British. When Jhansi was taken under British rule, Lakshmibai had to shift with her belongings to the city palace, where she would be under watch at all times. The army was disbanded and had to surrender their arms and uniform.

Her servants, too, lost their jobs. Small landowners lost their lands and had to take up petty clerical jobs in British offices. All of Gangadhar Rao's personal property and wealth was kept in a trust by the British, till Damodar Rao turned an adult and the Rani was deprived of it all, completely.

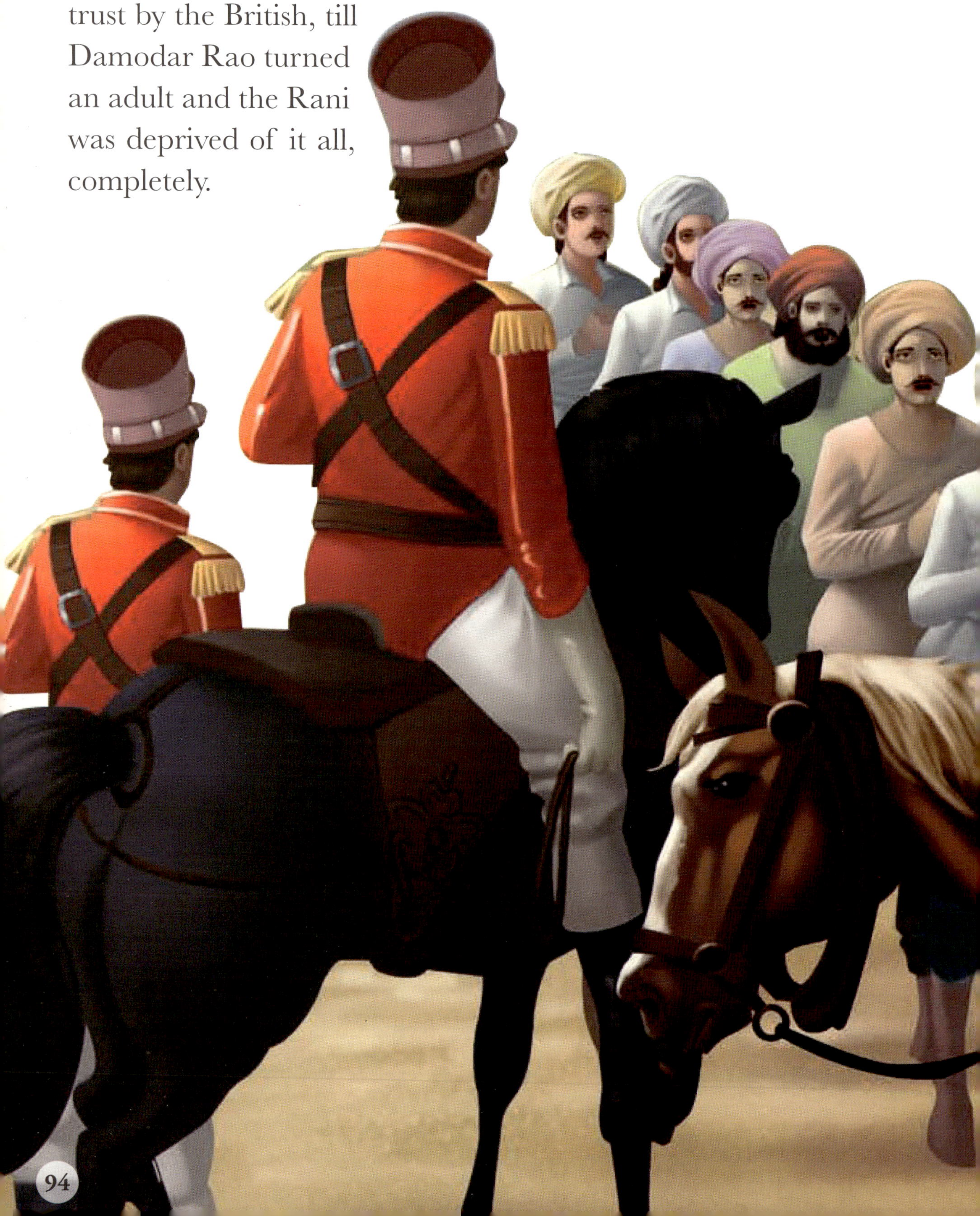

Since, Rani Lakshmibai was a widow, it was customary for her to live a life as simple as that of a hermit. Therefore, as per the Hindu Custom, Rani Lakshmibai's clothes and ornaments were to be sold in the market. Considering this as a chance to gain wealth, the British published the sale of Rani Lakshmibai's royal ornaments and belongings in their daily newspaper that was read only by the British Government. Some of the popular advertisement lines at that time had been: 'Buy the ornaments of Nagpur, buy the Naulakha necklace of Lucknow.'

The temples of Jhansi, including the Mahalakshmi temple, were taken over by the Company, too. They decided to stop all expenditure on religious ceremonies, calling it a waste of resources. This hurt the people's religious sentiments, deeply. Though Lakshmibai protested against this, she was told not to interfere. The biggest insult to the Hindus and Muslims of Jhansi was the new slaughter house,

set-up in the heart of the city. Pigs and cows were killed every day to prepare lavish meals for the British who lived in Jhansi. The Hindus worship the cow and the Muslims are forbidden to touch a pig, as per their customs. Thus, the activities of the slaughterhouse enraged the people. They became angrier and restless with each passing day. However, even through all the hardships, Lakshmibai always had the love and loyalty of her people.

While on one hand Rani Lakshmibai was preparing to regain control over Jhansi, Lord Dalhousie was exploiting Jhansi of all its riches and wealth. It began by downsizing the troops of the army of Jhansi and replacing the top Indian officials with the British commandant. Lord Dalhousie plundered the city to such an extent that its economy started to experience a steep downfall.

Fine carpets, brass articles and carved furniture that Jhansi was once famous for, were no more its pride. People were out of jobs; craftsmen, soldiers and shopkeepers were all idle. Looking at Jhansi's economy shrink, John Sullivan wrote, "with the disappearance of the native court, trade languished, the capital decayed, the people became impoverished while the Englishman flourished and acted like a sponge, drawing up riches from the Ganges and squeezing them down upon the banks of the Thames."

This meant that the British acted like a sponge, summing up Jhansi's wealth and delivering it to London at the cost of the life of the citizens of Jhansi. Although lawyer John Lang could sense the revolt that was bubbling underneath, it took a long while for other British officials to sense it.

The Durga Dal

Rani Lakshmibai continued to practise her skills with weapons and horses, all through the trying times. With time, she had gathered an army of women and had trained them to be as skilled as herself in the use of arms and to ride horses. Rani Lakshmibai had trained three women in

particular, Mandar, Sundar and Kashibai who were very loyal to her. In addition, many women from villages joined the woman-army. Soon, this army came to be known as the 'Durga Dal'. Among them was a very brave and strong woman named Jhalkari Bai. She had once killed a tiger with just an axe, when she was gathering firewood. It is said that she looked a lot like Lakshmibai and fought as valiantly as her.

Meanwhile, discontent had been rising in the public. People were very unhappy with the way the British Government treated them. They had become lords of the land and masters of the people. They even refused to give money out of Damodar Rao's trust fund for his 'sacred thread ceremony'. Slowly and steadily, the seeds of rebellion were sprouting everywhere.

False Blame

Finally, the revolt of 1857 occurred on 4 June triggered by the Sepoy regiment stationed at Jhansi. News had spread in a regiment of soldiers that the new cartridges provided to the army were smeared with animal fat. The Hindus were enraged as it was against their religion to eat meat. A sepoy or soldier named Mangal Pandey, a sepoy in Barrackpore in West Bengal, retaliated by shooting a British officer. The Government executed Mangal Pandey. Consequently, rebellion broke out. In Jhansi, too, the Indian sepoys of the British Army rebelled. The British officers and their families took shelter in the Jhansi Fort.

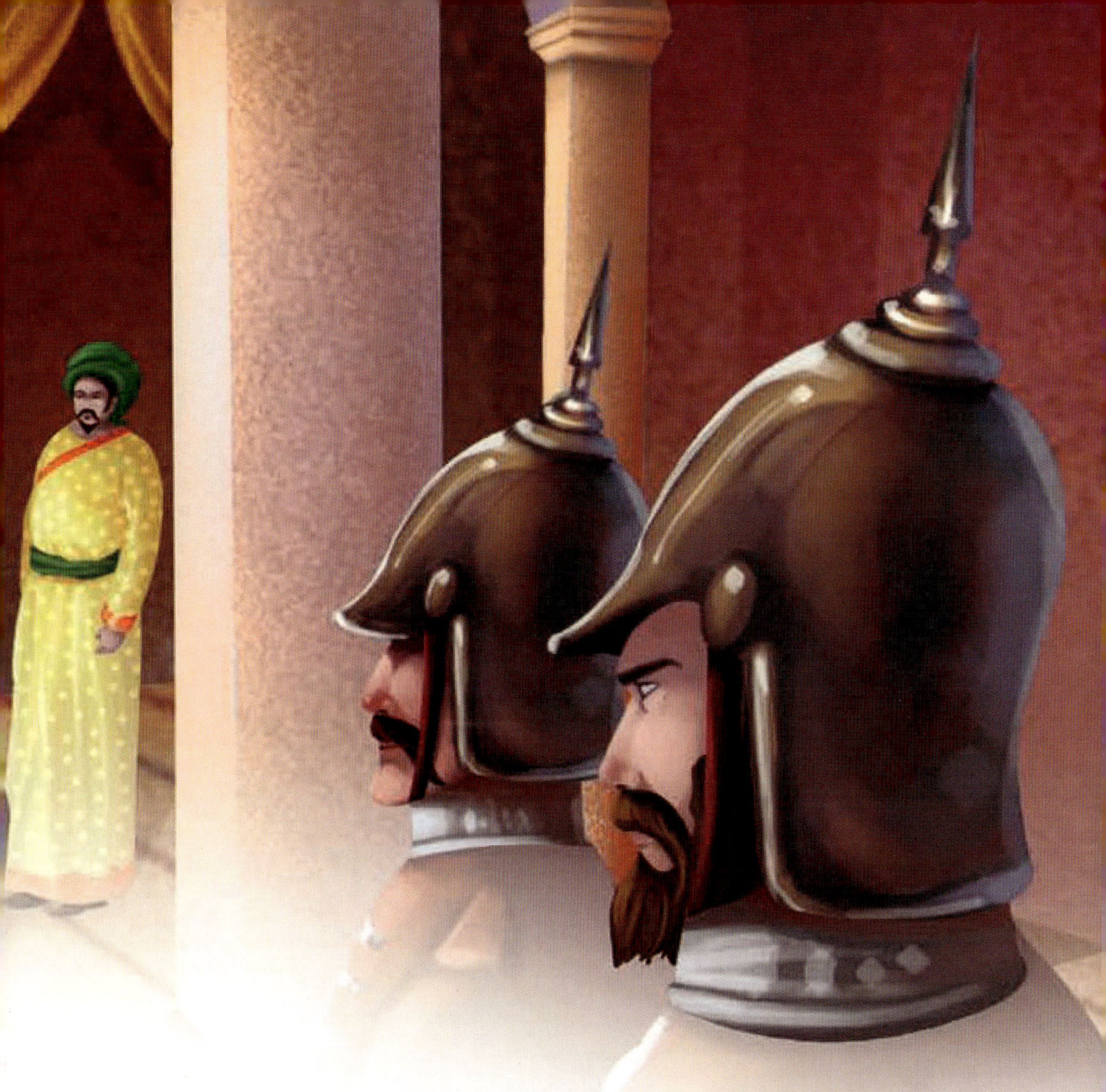

Rani Lakshmibai feared there would be bloodshed, so she advised the British to escape to another town, but they did not listen to her. Also, she could not protect them as the British had disbanded her army, when they had come into power. However, she did her best to help them out. She would send food and supplies to them through a secret tunnel, so that the women and children would not remain hungry. She also did her best to calm down the rebellion, but it was out of her control. She was shocked and shaken at the bloodbath, but had to appear confident, so that her people did not panic. However, unfortunately, all the British officers and even the women and children were murdered by the rebels.

Thereafter, the rebels asked Rani Lakshmibai to pay them a sum of three lakh rupees, as they had driven away the British from her kingdom. She had nothing to offer, but she wanted to stop the looting and fighting. So, she gave them the necklace she was wearing.

Ready for Battle

Meanwhile, once the British were pushed out of Jhansi after a fierce battle, Rani Lakshmibai became the ruler of Jhansi, once again. The people rejoiced and there was new confidence in their hearts. Durga Dal had become a strong force by then, an army of able warrior women, who were fiercely loyal to their Rani. The Queen assembled her army again.

A British officer, Colonel Martin had escaped safely from the fort. He informed the Government that the Rani had been of great help to them at the cost of danger to herself.

However, the Government blamed her for being responsible for the killings of their officers and their families at the Jhansi fort. Thus, they started calling her the 'Rebel Queen'. She was blamed without a hearing and a warrant was issued against her.

The prestigious Rajput clans of Bundela, Thakur and even Pathans, volunteered to be a part of the Rani's army. Her old friends, Nana Sahib and his brothers, and Tantiya Tope were also among many of her allies. The arms and ammunitions that had been hidden away, were taken out and cleaned. Among them all was the famous cannon, Karakbijli. It had a lion's head at its mouth and was said to have had the longest range any cannon ever had at that time. In the past, these cannon had made the enemy armies flee in no time from Jhansi. Moreover, new weapons were also being manufactured. The Rani prepared for the final battle against the British. For, she knew they would strike, soon.

The Fearsome Battle

The Rani's apprehension was right. Soon, the British Army, led by General Rose, attacked Jhansi. However, the Rani had prepared Jhansi well. The fort had twenty-feet thick granite walls that were difficult to break through. A deep ditch surrounded another part of the boundary, making it impossible to cross over to the fort. Five cannons were stationed to throw a rapid volley of cannon balls, which destroyed all that stood in their way. Rani Lakshmibai's army had very skilled Pathan artillerymen. Even the British soldiers praised their skills and were no match for them.

At the battlefield, Lieutenant Rose was eager to fight a woman as brave as a man. When his forces came against those of Rani Lakshmibai's, he saw the bold Queen stand tall and strong ahead of her army of brave men. As the two armies clashed, Lieutenant Rose tried getting closer to Rani Lakshmibai in order to wage an attack on her. When Rani Lakshmibai saw Lieutenant Rose closing on to her, she drew and swung her sword with such courage and aggression that the Lieutenant, without waiting for a minute, retreated from the battlefield with his army. Not expecting a Queen to display such courage on the field, Lieutenant Rose could not stop himself from admiring Rani Lakshmibai's agility and prowess.

For a long time, the Rani's army kept up a strong defence. They were able to destroy many weapons, cannons and soldiers of the British Army. But soon, General Rose was able to create havoc in Jhansi, as he fired his cannons, destroying the city and creating panic among the people. Rani Lakshmibai's women soldiers fought as bravely as the men. A woman named Bakshin took charge of the guns. Later, she fell martyr during the battle. Many of the Rani's strongest comrades fell in the battle.

Finally, the British entered the city. They looted and plundered, setting fire to the palace, the theatre, the library and everything of importance. Many children and women died. At this point, the Queen suffered a moment of weakness. She decided to commit suicide with her loyal women warriors. However, a leader of her army, Tatya Tope convinced her to remain strong for her son, Damodar.

Rani Lakshmibai felt sorry for her moment of weakness. She decided to escape to Kalpi and fight alongside the Peshwa, there. She rode her favourite horse, Sarangi, with young Damodar strapped onto her back. In the past, when Rani Lakshmibai was in trouble, she called out to Rao Sahib in Kalpi for help. However, he had not reached her with support, this time. Thus, Rani Lakshmibai was very angry. Rao Sahib was embarrassed and apologetic and begged her to fight with them. For the Rani, it was important to put aside any anger and fight alongside her fellow countrymen for the motherland. Thereafter, harsh battles continued at Kalpi and the surrounding areas, for a long time. Many allies and armies joined the Peshwa and the Rani. Even then, they were no match for the well-trained British soldiers. One after the other, the armies fell or fled. The British Army was soon victorious.

A Hero Dies

After their failure, the rebels did not disband and disappear. They took refuge in Gwalior, to build up their strength again. Among the rebels were Tantiya Tope, Rani Lakshmibai, Rao Sahib and Nawab of Banda. When the British came to know about the rebels' hiding place, they planned to attack, at once. Thereafter, the British Army attacked Gwalior from several points. The courageous rebels put up a brave fight. Rani Lakshmibai entrusted her son Damodar in the care of her loyal friends and set out to the battlefield. She had lost her favourite horse, Sarangi, in the earlier battle. Now she chose another fine horse, dressed in the uniform of a Gwalior soldier, and rushed to the fight, with her loyal

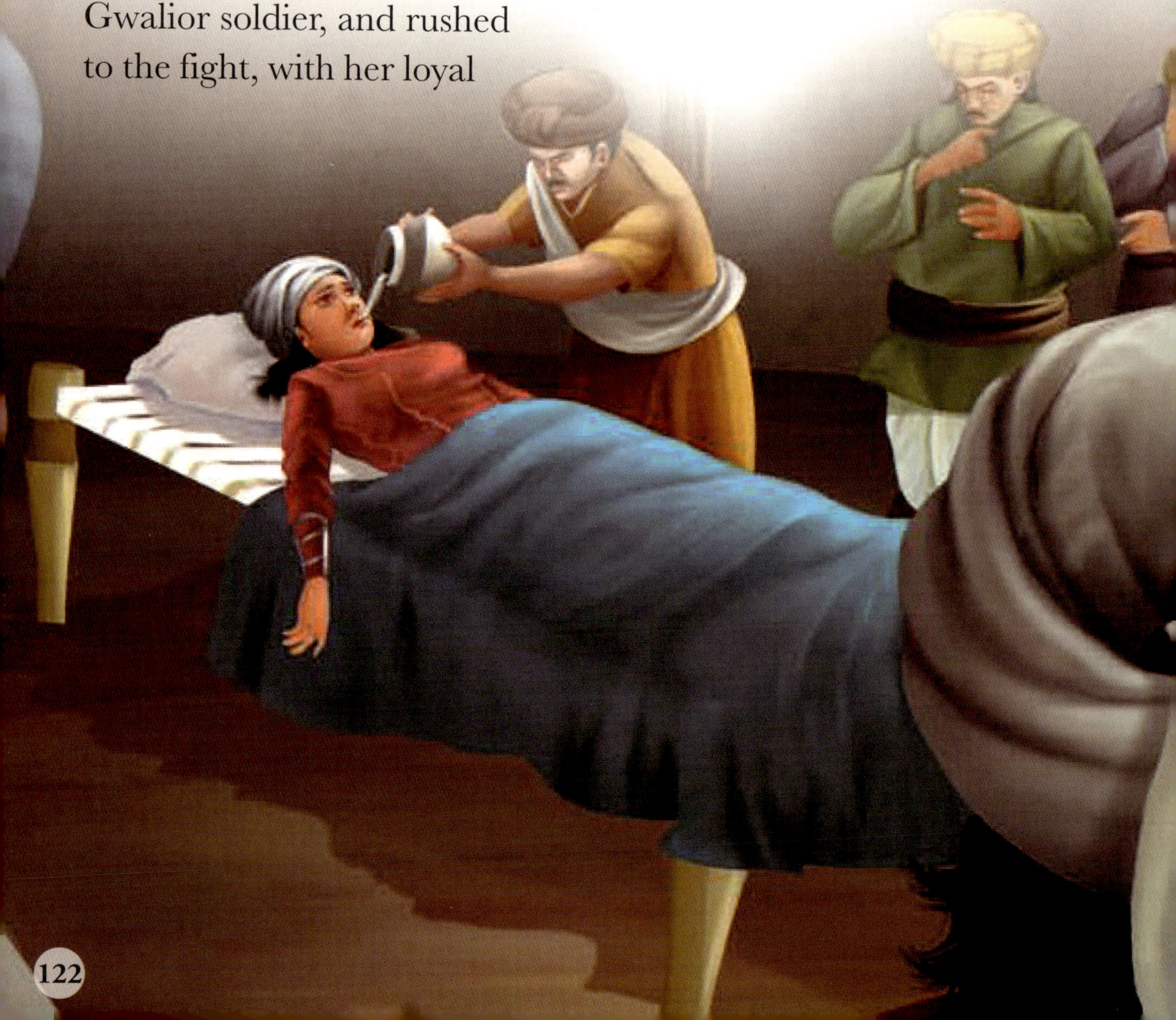

soldiers, Mandar and Raghunath Singh. It is said that in the course of the fight, an enemy soldier hit Mandar. She called out to her Rani, "Bai Sahiba, I've been hit!" Rani Lakshmibai, at once, swung around on her horse and attacked Mandar's assailant and killed him with a flash of her sword. Sadly, just then, she was attacked from behind. A sword slashed at her head and a bullet pierced her chest. She fell forward on her horse and was separated from her comrades.

After some time, the soldiers found her bleeding on her horse. They took her to an ascetic's hut and poured Gangajal into her parched mouth.

Her end was near and with a cry of 'Har Har Mahadev,' the valiant Rani Lakshmibai died. All those who loved her, drowned in grief, but they kept up the rebellion she had given her life for.

Soon after, within a few days, Rani Lakshmibai's father Moropant Tambe was also captured and executed by the British.

Some people believe that one of the great warriors from her army – Raghunath Singh had made quick arrangements for her funeral on the same day as she died. He had discreetly made sure that Rani Lakshmibai was given her last farewell with all rights and ceremonies at the spot where she was wounded and killed.

However, when Captain Reese inspected the battlefield after the war, a low number of casualties made him believe that Rani Lakshmibai had fled from the fight and was alive. With this belief, he made a statement to the public, saying that the Rani was alive.

Meanwhile, Damodar Rao (originally named Anand Rao), under the custody of Rani Lakshmibai's friend, moved from one place to another, hiding from the British. When found, he underwent trial and was finally freed of all charges against him. The British Government gave him some pension, but denied him the right to inheritance. Damodar later settled in Indore and fought unsuccessfully all his life with the British to win back his inheritance. But in view of his royal lineage his descendents took on the last name of Jhansiwale.

General Sir Hugo Rose, who was constantly waging war against Rani Lakshmibai, and was on numerous occasions defeated by her till he had his final victory, was also a witness to her greatness and aweinspiring personality. His words for Rani Lakshmibai were, "Of the mutineers the bravest and the greatest commander was the Rani."

Rani Lakshmibai is an epitome of courage, bravery and wisdom for all Indian men and women. With her modern thought, backed by dedicated actions, she came as a boon to all women hailing from the 19th century. Lakshmibai will never be forgotten. She lives on as a brave hero in the heart of every Indian.

The memory of Rani Lakshmibai is immortalised in bronze statues that are placed at Jhansi and Gwalior. The statues show her sitting on a horse, holding a sword in her hand.

Jao Rani yaad rakhengey yeh krutagna Bharatwasi,

Yeh tera balidaan jagavega swatantrata avinasi,

Hovey chup itihaas, lagey sachchai ko chahey phansi,

Ho madmaati vijay, mitaa dey golon sey chahey Jhansi.

Tera smarak tu hi hogi, tu khud amit nishaani thi,

Bundeley harbolon key munh hamney suni kahani thi,

Khoob ladi mardani woh to Jhansi wali rani thi.

O! Rani Lakshmibai, we, the grateful people of India will always hold your sacrifice for the nation in great esteem. Your debt will never be forgotten.

Your sacrifice has awakened an indestructible fire for freedom in the people of our country.

History may be silenced, the truth be hanged or Jhansi be destroyed with cannonballs or the enemy is drunk with victory, You, Rani Lakshmibai, will always remain alive in our heart and spirit.

Thoughts of you will serve as your memorial, since you have given us the eternal token of courage.

The tale of her courage is narrated in the songs sung by the religious singers of Bundelkhand.

They speak of her gallantry that no man could equal, and how her spirit reverberated for freedom from the British intruders.

Such was the Queen of Jhansi!